FIFTY-TWO WORDS
MY HUSBAND TAUGHT ME

FIFTY-TWO WORDS MY HUSBAND TAUGHT ME

LOVE, INSPIRATION AND THE CONSTITUTION

JOY RODINO

Library of Congress Control Number: 2008910430
ISBN: 9780615259383

Cover concept by Scott Jacobs
Cover design by Partners in Design
Cover photographs by Steven Polansky

DRJ Publishing Inc.
West Orange, NJ

Printed in the United States of America

www.PeterRodino.com

CONTENTS

To Peter

with love, and great respect

ACKNOWLEDGMENTS

I am deeply grateful to Shar McBee, who inspired me to write this book, for her insight, advice, enthusiasm and encouragement every step along the way, and to Professor Bill Berlin, whose mutually heartfelt connection with Peter led to many months of recorded interviews. Together with my personal conversations, they provided the basis for the anecdotes in this account.

Peter inspired his congressional staffers, and I would like to express my appreciation for their unfailing devotion to him over the years. Special thanks to Skip Endres, Alan Parker, Sandy Sincavitz, Larry Spinelli and the late Tony Suriano, Peter's longtime district office manager and close friend, who gave new meaning to the word *loyal*.

I am equally grateful to Peter's devoted Seton Hall Law School colleagues: Merilee Jennings, the first archivist to work on my husband's congressional papers, for her professionalism, dedication and guidance; Professor Judson

Jennings, Peter's co-teacher, whose intellectual and personal support enabled Peter to continue teaching and inspiring students to his final days; and his protégé, Professor Paula Franzese, the current holder of the Rodino endowed chair, for her good heart, and for carrying forth Peter's legacy.

To our special friends and extended family, thank you for your support and for being so generous with your wisdom and advice: Judge Paul Armstrong, Scott and Pat Chesney, Natalie and Stanley Elman, Deborah Fennelly, Dr. Joseph and Lucille Fennelly, Dr. Mojdeh Haghverdi, Dr. Gladys Hirschorn, Darlene Hart, Kim Ragoni, Marcie Rose and Dr. Helen Strauss. My heartfelt thanks to my dear friend Joyce Hanula, for her optimism and support and for being such an inspiration. To my loving family, particularly Karen Levine, Gail Feinstein and Leonard Judelson, my deepest gratitude for your encouragement and meaningful advice, and a special thanks to Amy Levine Herman for introducing us to *What Will Matter* and Steven Polansky for his beautiful photographs. Thanks also to Sarah Conduragis, Mary Gamba, Richard Gillette and Jonathan Shimkin for their guidance, and Michael Bernoff for inspiring me to take action and live my vision.

To my astute editors, April Allridge and Connie Buchanan, and to the Winthrop Group, especially Linda Edgerly and archivists Bonnie Sauer and Jed Winokur, for their expertise and care in processing the Rodino papers, a special thank you.

Above all, I would like to express my deepest gratitude to and love for my spiritual teacher, who showed me the way.

PREFACE

This is a story about honor and integrity, courage and respect, but mostly it is a story about love—about my late husband's deep, abiding love and reverence for the Preamble to the Constitution of the United States, and how his lifelong dedication to its guiding principles inspired me and so many in our nation.

For forty years my husband, Peter W. Rodino, Jr., represented the Tenth District of New Jersey as a member of the United States House of Representatives. People remember him best for his role as chairman of the House Judiciary Committee in guiding the inquiry into whether President Richard Nixon committed high crimes and misdemeanors against the United States. During that crucial time in our country's history, Peter's unwavering adherence to an impartial quest for the truth resulted in a bipartisan committee vote recommending that the president be impeached. A single conviction steered his conduct at that time and throughout his life: the United States, founded upon the Constitution, is a nation of laws, and no man is above the law—not even the most powerful person in the world.

During his career Peter interacted with presidents, popes, kings and queens, but he remained first and foremost a man of the people. As a "constituent Congressman" intent on serving the residents of the Tenth District, he helped people with problems large and small, issues ranging from military service and housing to healthcare and federal benefits. I should know. Forty-five years ago, after graduating from Smith College with a B.A. in political science, I went to work for Congressman Rodino in Washington, D.C., spending six years as his executive assistant and office manager. I will never forget him saying that when he first took the oath of office, he asked himself what he could do as a representative of the people. How could he best serve his constituents? Decades later and three years after his passing, New Jerseyans still approach me in public to tell me how Peter personally touched their lives.

During my years in his office, Congressman Rodino— that is what I called him back then—used to reminisce about his love of writing and poetry. In high school, he said, he steeped himself in Shakespeare, Byron, Coleridge and Whitman, committing to memory his favorite passages, many of which he could still recite. As a young man he was intent on widening his vocabulary and improving his ability to converse intelligently. His ritual was to learn five new words a day, then use the words in conversation. After reading about Demosthenes, the great orator who as a youth put pebbles in his mouth to learn to enunciate more clearly, Peter stuffed his own mouth with pebbles and walked around Branch Brook Park, a 360-acre oasis across the street from the tenement house in Newark where he grew up, reciting the poetry he had memorized. From an early age, he had a poetic, philosophical nature that would eventually find full expression in his career in Washington.

After working in Washington I moved to Massachusetts, then decided to go to law school. In 1974 I was about to begin Northeastern University School of Law. Having been out of college for ten years, I was somewhat apprehensive about returning to academia. What helped me was watching Congressman Rodino as the new chairman of the House Judiciary Committee rise to the challenge presented by the Watergate inquiry. That gave me courage to face my own, much smaller challenge. "Yes I can" became my motto, and I wrote the congressman to thank him for being a role model as I entered this new phase of my life.

In the ensuing years our paths crossed occasionally when I visited Washington. Almost twenty years would go by, however, before our destinies converged. By then I was a public-interest attorney and he was chairman of the House Judiciary Committee, having made the transition from constituent congressman to national hero and defender of the Constitution. A former colleague asked me to speak to the congressman about a legislative issue. It was 1987. His first wife, Ann, had passed away seven years earlier. We married in 1989, just as Peter retired from Congress and began his new career as a professor at Seton Hall University School of Law.

That was when I first heard Peter express his admiration for what five of our Founding Fathers were able to accomplish over the course of six short days: drafting the fifty-two words that would become the Preamble to the Constitution. To him, the Constitution was the heart of our nation, the mechanism that gave life to the system under which we live, a government of checks and balances, of rights and responsibilities. The Preamble was our country's soul, not only projecting a vision of who we are as a people but also expressing the limitless possibilities of all that we can be:

> We the people of the United States, in order to form a more perfect union, establish justice, insure domestic tranquility, provide for the common defense, promote the general welfare, and secure the blessings of liberty to ourselves and our posterity, do ordain and establish this Constitution for the United States of America.

Those fifty-two words were as sacred to my husband as the Bible. He made reference to them in every discussion he had about politics and the state of the world, in every speech he gave and in every class he led.

Peter inspired his students to live by the highest ideals and to make a difference in the lives of others. Even at the ripe age of ninety-five, he would come home from teaching energized by his interaction with his pupils. During one class a student asked: "Professor, in your opinion, what makes our country so unique? What is the glue that keeps it together?"

Without hesitation Peter replied, "The blessings of liberty." Yes, the blessings of liberty.

Shortly after 9/11 Peter received an e-mail with a quote from a moving editorial, "Ode to America," which had been published in a Romanian newspaper. Peter cited this in several of his speeches, because it captures the essence of what he himself felt, his passionate dedication to the uplifting vision of our Founding Fathers:

> Why are Americans so united? They don't resemble one another even if you paint them! They speak all the languages of the world and form an astonishing mixture of civilizations. Some of them are nearly extinct, others are incompatible with one another, and in matters of religious beliefs, not even God can count how many they are. Still, the American

tragedy turned three hundred million people into a hand put on the heart.... The Americans volunteered to donate blood and to give a helping hand. After the first moments of panic, they raised the flag on the smoking ruins, putting on T-shirts, caps and ties in the colors of the national flag. They placed flags on buildings and cars as if in every place and in every car a minister or the president was passing. On every occasion they started singing ... "God Bless America!"

...What on earth can unite the Americans in such a way? Their land? Their galloping history? Their economic power? ... I tried for hours to find an answer.... I thought things over, but I reached only one conclusion. Only freedom can work such miracles![1]

Peter dedicated his entire career to preserving the foundation of freedom upon which our nation is built. Indeed, the very purpose of his life was "to leave the Constitution as unimpaired for our children as our predecessors left it for us."[2] In memory of my husband, then, and to share with you some of the myriad ways in which his words and actions supported his purpose, I turn to the Preamble.

WE THE PEOPLE OF THE UNITED STATES, IN ORDER TO FORM A MORE PERFECT UNION

Before my discussions with Peter, I had never really contemplated the origins of the Constitution. Listening to him helped me better grasp the enormity of what our forefathers accomplished in 1787. "When fifty-five delegates assembled in Philadelphia two hundred years ago," he said in a speech commemorating the Bicentennial of the Constitution,

> they had no intention of producing a new constitutional document. They met to revise the Articles of Confederation, which had proven woefully inadequate in holding together thirteen small but fiercely independent republics.

But their revision efforts never materialized. Instead, during a ferociously hot Philadelphia summer, stormy debates ensued that reopened the question of just what the "grand experiment" of '76 was supposed to produce in practice. It was a difficult period of self-examination; a third of the delegates simply gave up and returned home…. The "127-day ordeal," as Madison later referred to it, ended with agreements on a four-page, handwritten document that changed the course of world history forever.

…In this single paragraph [the Preamble], the framers succeeded in establishing the democratic framework of our new republic. It was to be a government as concerned about the general welfare of its people as about the common defense. It was to be a government dedicated to bringing justice and the blessings of liberty not to just one class or group, but to all the people—and not just for the present, but for our posterity.

But the vision and promise of the new republic was not immediately apparent to all the assembled delegates…. The proceedings reveal that the precise phrasing, syntax and form of the Preamble underwent more drafts and revisions than some of the very detailed articles that follow....

The so-called Committee of Five—Doctor Johnson, Alexander Hamilton, Gouverneur Morris, James Madison and Rufus King—took the draft, went into seclusion, revised it over the course of six days, and finally returned to the delegates with a brand new version. It was "a remarkable transformation," Peter went on, for

> no longer did the Preamble narrowly refer to the people as only citizens of the [thirteen individual states]. Instead, the Preamble spoke of "we the people of the United States, in order to form a more perfect union." No longer did the Preamble contain a ... statement of intent, whose unconcealed purpose was to diffuse tensions among the states. The Preamble now expounded the very reasons for government. Such a pronouncement, impossible at the beginning of the convention, was accepted without question at its end.
>
> As I have thought of this history, I continue to marvel at two aspects of the final language adopted by the Founding Fathers. The first is that balance—a kind of dynamic equilibrium—is the hallmark of the "more perfect union" sought by our Founding Fathers. Once liberated from purely parochial concerns,

they devoted themselves to the multiple, over-lapping goals inherent in a free society: "to establish justice, insure domestic tranquility, provide for the common defense, promote the general welfare..."

All of these avowed purposes for forming the new republic must necessarily dovetail if the system is to work....

The second aspect of the Preamble by which I am struck is the unmistakable presence of a *covenant of trust*: "We the people of the United States in order to form a more perfect union..." These [words] are ... a social compact between the people and each other and the government. Any breach of that covenant threatens the very foundation of our democracy.[3]

And a breach did occur, during the Watergate break-in in early 1972. It proved to be the source of the greatest constitutional crisis that our nation has ever endured. Though questions arose about whether the president had been involved in the break-in, Nixon was re-elected. The following year several members of the House introduced legislation calling for his impeachment. Under the Constitution, any impeachment inquiry is conducted solely under the jurisdiction of the House. As a matter of course, the Speaker of the House assigned the bill to the

Judiciary Committee, which has jurisdiction over all matters relating to the Constitution.

For many years Peter had been the second-ranking Democrat on the House Judiciary Committee. Now, as its newly appointed chairman—replacing long-time head Emanuel Celler, who had served in the House for almost fifty years—he had to call upon all of his inner and outer resources. The magnitude of this new responsibility weighed heavily on Peter. He received many letters impugning his integrity. Some people assumed that since he was of Italian origin, he must be associated with the mafia. And questions arose among his colleagues as to whether he possessed the strength and leadership ability to lead the committee in this ground-breaking work. After all, he was a brand new chairman, and no impeachment inquiry had been conducted in over a hundred years. Despite the pressure, Peter guided the committee through its historic inquiry with caution, evenhandedness and a dedication to the truth, thereby leaving an enduring legacy for our nation.

From his earliest years, Peter had had a sense that he was destined to play a significant role in our nation's history. When he was a child his parents would take him to saints-day celebrations in Newark's North Ward, where the family lived surrounded by Italian immigrants striving for a better life. The statue of a patron saint from a specific region of Italy would be paraded through tenement-lined streets, accompanied by a band playing Italian marches and followed by throngs of immigrants from that region. After the procession the musicians would move to a bandstand in the piazza next to St. Lucy's Church and entertain the crowd with popular Italian songs and arias. The celebration would last through the night, a warm, exuberant gathering, the air filled with the aroma of traditional sausage, peppers and *zeppole*. On one such occasion, little Peter was in his mother's arms watching the maestro conducting the band. Suddenly he began to wave his own arms about. "Look at him," Mrs. Rodino said to her husband, "he's waving a baton. He's going to be somebody—he's going to be a leader." Mrs. Rodino passed away from tuberculosis when her son was only four. According to Peter, her intuition about his leadership potential, as recounted to him by his father, was the driving force in his life.

Peter also remembered the strong guidance his father provided while he was growing up. He revered his father, a multitalented man—artist, master carpenter, woodcarver, sculptor and painter—who worked for thirty-seven years at the Hyatt Roller Bearing Company as a designer and head toolmaker. It was the strength of his father's character, and the lessons he imparted, that shaped the man of integrity Peter would become. His father always emphasized that while it was important to become somebody, Peter was not to aspire to a position for the sake of money or his ego. "He would talk to me," Peter said, about people who had pulled themselves up from humble beginnings and served the public. He encouraged me to keep studying, and to remember that I should live a life of decency, integrity, honesty and honor, always striving to make a difference in the lives of others.

I remember one Christmas, during the Depression, when we were really in bad shape and the holidays were bleak, my father gave my sister, brother and me envelopes in which he had enclosed for each of us a two-dollar bill. On the flap of each envelope he had written the words "Be Eppie." I've never forgotten those words and what they mean. That vision of my father counseling us to be happy with the blessings that really mattered had a great deal to do with what I have become. I wanted to emulate his character.[4]

As the impeachment inquiry began, Peter remembered those words of his father that had instilled in him a high moral standard and respect for people in authority. As he told me, "The last thing I wanted to do was to impeach the president and hold him responsible for misdeeds which would have caused us to remove him from office."[5] Peter said that he venerated the office of the president and that it was important that he not be viewed as the

"Democratic" chairman. He had to demonstrate both by word and by deed his impartiality.

Peter hired John Doar to lead the impeachment inquiry. Doar's name had been submitted by many people—judges, lawyers, academics and others—from whom Peter had solicited recommendations. Doar had a strong record at the civil rights division of the Justice Department, a reputation for courage, independence and integrity, and deep respect for the Constitution. After his final interview with Doar, Peter said,

> I'm going to hire you, and you're going to have the responsibility of conducting this investigation…. You'll be the one who will set up the whole committee staff. You will have my complete confidence, but you must remember that I have veto power over all of it. And there is one other thing that I'm going to insist upon, and that is that we're going to conduct this investigation thoroughly, completely, and be satisfied that there are no loopholes.[6]

Peter told Doar not to talk to the press, and never to offer an opinion regarding the grounds for impeachment until they had all the facts and they could come to a conclusion supported by the evidence. If Doar displayed any partisanship or offered any opinion that wasn't corroborated, he would be fired. Peter stressed that Doar should select all the people on his committee staff with the same kind of caveat—if anyone breached that rule, they would be let go.

When Peter held a press conference announcing Doar's appointment, he received a note from someone seated in the audience: Melvin Laird, former secretary of defense under Nixon. "Pete, a wonderful appointment," the note said. "Did you know that John Doar was a Republican appointed by Eisenhower?"[7] No, Peter hadn't been aware of Doar's party affiliation. Above all, he was determined to conduct the proceedings impartially.

While the Constitution gives to the House of Representatives the sole power of impeachment, Peter wanted to ensure the authority of the Judiciary Committee to undertake this momentous task. On February 6, 1974, he went before the House to ask its consent to a resolution explicitly authorizing the Judiciary Committee to conduct the impeachment inquiry and to provide the committee with the power of subpoena. Against all precedents, the resolution provided that the chairman and the ranking minority member would share the authority to issue subpoenas, a move intended to underscore the bipartisan spirit in which Peter intended to conduct the inquiry. "We know that the real security of this nation lies in the integrity of its institutions and the informed confidence of its people," he said to his colleagues in the House. "We will conduct our deliberations in that spirit."[8] Peter concluded his remarks by quoting Thomas Paine:

"Those who expect to reap the blessings of freedom must, like men, undergo the fatigue of supporting it."

For almost two hundred years, Americans have undergone the stress of preserving their freedom and the Constitution that protects it. It is our turn now.

We are going to work expeditiously and fairly....

Whatever the result, whatever we learn or conclude, let us now proceed, with such care and decency and thoroughness and honor that the vast majority of the American people, and their children after them, will say: That was the right course. There was no other way.[9]

Early support came from an unexpected source. One day Peter received a phone call from Senator John Stennis, the revered and powerful chairman of the Senate Armed Services Committee. The senator's colleagues regarded him as a genuine Southern gentleman, a venerable patrician and true patriot. He and Peter had never met. "The senator said he'd like to come over and discuss with me a matter of greatest importance," Peter recounted.

I opened the door of my office and warmly ushered him in. He said, "Mr. Chairman, I won't take up much of your time, but I had to see you. There comes a time when a country is in crisis. One of those times is now, and fate calls on someone to deal with that crisis. I believe that fate has called on you." I said, "Mr. Chairman, don't say that! It feels like the weight of the world is on me."

He said he wanted to make sure I knew that people like him had complete faith and trust in me.

That affirmation from Senator Stennis had a powerful impact on Peter as he steered the committee on its quest for the truth. The facts, he hoped, would show that the president had not breached his covenant with the people. However, Peter accepted the awesome responsibility of ensuring that the committee made a decision based on whatever facts surfaced in the investigation.

An important defining moment for Peter came during a speech, given extemporaneously, before a breakfast reception of the Army-Navy Union, a New Jersey veterans' organization. To his surprise the organizers informed him that he would be receiving an award. Instead of the forty people he had expected, a crowd of over three hundred people had assembled. Peter was well aware that most veterans supported the president and were opposed to impeachment. He was also mindful of the mail he had been receiving, full of threatening messages calling him a traitor and saying that he would be responsible for dividing the country if the president were impeached.

As he contemplated what to say to the large gathering, suddenly it dawned on him: these were veterans who had fought for their country, as he had. They had sacrificed for the very principles that had ensured the nation's survival. That was what was at stake. He would have to impress upon them that he was "under an obligation to inquire, not to pre-condemn," that it was his responsibility to preserve the institutions for which many had given their lives and to ensure that our democracy wasn't being jeopardized by the president.[10]

Peter shared with the audience a letter he had recently received from the parents of two children, members of the generation that would "inherit this land."[11] They told him that while watching television one day, their children had heard the president say, "I'm not a crook." They asked their parents whether this was true. The parents didn't know the answer to the question; it was the congressman's responsibility, they wrote, to discover the truth. This poignant anecdote helped Peter convey to the veterans that indeed this was his duty.

While Peter was proud to be a Democrat, the question of how he could best serve the people remained first and foremost in his mind. He was adamant that the word *inquiry* be used rather than *investigation*. "That meant," said Peter, "that we had to look at all the inculpatory and exculpatory evidence as the basis for finding whether or not sufficient grounds existed to remove a president from office, and those who would ultimately decide how we handled ourselves were the people of the United States."

The Constitution states that "the President ... shall be removed from Office on Impeachment for, and Conviction of, Treason, Bribery, or other high Crimes and Misdemeanors." In February 1974 the Judiciary Committee received a staff report, "Constitutional Grounds for Presidential Impeachment," which examined the historical context of impeachment and considered what the framers meant by "high crimes and misdemeanors." The report concluded that "impeachment is a constitutional remedy [whose scope is limited to removal from office and possible disqualification from future office] addressed to serious offenses against the system of government."[12] Historically, when articles of impeachment have been considered, the "emphasis has been on the significant effects of the conduct—undermining the integrity of office, disregard of constitutional duties and oath of office, arrogation of power, abuse of the governmental process, adverse impact on the system of government."[13] This report would serve as an important frame of reference for committee members when they subsequently assessed the evidence brought before them.

From the beginning of the inquiry, many Democrats who favored a fast political solution said that Peter was moving too slowly, delaying the process—that he was going to let everything go down the drain. At one point he received a dressing down from Tip O'Neill, the House majority leader. "Tippy" was an early mentor of Peter's, a man he held in the highest regard. When the majority leader began prodding him to pick up the pace, he listened quietly before saying, "Are you done?" And then Peter, who was never known to curse, said, "Tippy, go f— yourself." Intent on conducting the process correctly and thoroughly, Peter was already exhausted by the clamor from his own party.

Statistics reflect the meticulous nature of the committee's approach. Its staff presented the committee with 650 "statements of information" (facts pointing to grounds for impeachment) and over 7,200 pages of evidentiary material, inculpatory as well as exculpatory, which the members reviewed in executive session. They also heard recordings of nineteen presidential conversations and took testimony from nine witnesses. Throughout this process, conducted under the so-called Rodino rules, Peter insisted that confidentiality be maintained and that the staff present no conclusions—not even opinions—to the committee.

All the committee members felt the strain of the inquiry. A good friend, Congressman Walter Flowers, a Democrat from Alabama with whom Peter regularly played paddleball in the House gym, agonized over the fact that his constituency strongly supported Nixon. Congressman Flowers, Peter told me, was putting his whole soul into arriving at a fair, honest and just decision. So was Congressman Tom Railsbeck, a Republican and good friend of the president. As he became increasingly aware of the fact that Nixon had betrayed the public trust, Congressman Railsbeck's face couldn't hide his torment. He told Peter that he could hardly hold up his head if he didn't do what he felt was right, painful as it might be.[14]

In late July 1974, the committee held a televised debate about whether to recommend a resolution, together with articles of impeachment, to impeach the president of the United States. There were three articles of impeachment, charging that one, the president had acted to cover up the Watergate break-in; two, he had abused the powers of his office; and three, he had obstructed justice. Peter recalled that when, in a hushed voice, he voted aye to recommend impeachment on the first article, he felt completely drained. At the conclusion of that historic vote, he adjourned the meeting, bypassed all the reporters and staff, went into his little office off the committee room, and called his wife. "Ann," he said, "I guess you heard." And he put the phone down and burst into tears.

In anguish, "we the people" had spoken. The "more perfect union," a nation of laws, not of men, had been preserved.

ESTABLISH JUSTICE, INSURE DOMESTIC TRANQUILITY

When they included in the Preamble the words "establish justice," Peter maintained, our forefathers recognized the need to guarantee "equal treatment of equals," to establish a system that "renders to each citizen the rights due him or her," a system in which "freedom is limited only as regulated by justice." Justice could not be established without a structural foundation: a system of legislators, courts and agencies to enforce the law.

In Peter's mind, the clause "insure domestic tranquility" meant that "the government must set up a system of protection which respects the right of each individual to express himself or herself, and which allows each to enjoy the rights of life, liberty and happiness without infringing on the rights of others." Americans should understand that the Founding Fathers "gave voice to the common aim of the people by establishing the framework which would provide guidelines for each individual to respect, a way to live an ordered life in an ordered society." Peter believed that domestic tranquility would only be possible through the establishment of an authorized force, the police, and the provision of the means for civil dissent. The police would maintain order; allowing dissent would prevent outbreaks of violence.

At age seventeen, when he was a senior in high school, Peter had his own firsthand experience of the breakdown of the Founding Fathers' ideals. It was New Year's Eve. He and a friend, nicely dressed in suits and fedoras, were leaving a midnight party at Loews Theater on Broad Street in Newark. "As we were walking home," Peter recalled,

> the streets were still alive with people. The store windows were lit up with beautiful Christmas scenes, and we stopped along the way to look at the decorations. Suddenly, I heard a thud. I looked back and saw that two automobiles had been in an accident, and a crowd of people had gathered around. It didn't appear that anyone was hurt, and I started to go on my way.
>
> I hadn't gone more than fifty feet when, upon rounding a turn, I saw two policemen coming. I glanced at one of the policemen. Seeing that his cap was skewed and his hair disheveled, I thought that he might be

intoxicated. He was over six feet tall, wearing the standard blue uniform and a long gray coat, and he had one of those billy clubs hanging on the side. The other officer was older and shorter. I hadn't passed them by more than five feet when I heard the taller, disheveled one say, "Hey, come here!" in a commanding tone of voice. I turned around, and he beckoned.

His friend didn't budge, but Peter, who had always been taught to respect authority, approached the policeman. Before he reached him, the policeman mumbled something. Apparently the man thought Peter had insulted him, uttering an Italian curse that meant "Go f— yourself!" The sentence was barely out of the policeman's mouth when,

> without giving me an opportunity to reply, he came at me with the billy club and smashed me right over the nose. I reeled, and I could feel a rush of blood starting to come out. Then he hit me again. I could feel my teeth loosen and my hat came off. I could do nothing except grab onto him, and I put my arms around his waist. As I felt myself falling, I remember trying to find his gun.
>
> The older policeman immediately said,

"What the hell are you doing? Stop it!" and he pulled me away. I remember getting my handkerchief out to wipe my face. It immediately became drenched with blood, and I dropped it right there at the curb. All the people in the crowd were gasping, but no one came to my assistance. The only thing they did afterwards was to pick up my blood-stained hat. My friend had fled, and there was no one there to assist me.

Peter remembered the policeman's name from his badge. He dragged himself up Seventh Avenue, went into the police station in that precinct, and with his bloodied face announced to the desk sergeant that he wanted to make a complaint. He told him what had happened and mentioned the officer's name. The sergeant just gave him a cursory glance and replied, "Get out of here—you're probably one of those rowdy kids." It was a stinging response that Peter never forgot.

Most of police officers in the North Ward were of Irish or German background, and most of the residents were Italian. Unfortunately, Peter told me,

in the eyes of many non-Italians, if you came from Little Italy, it was assumed you were connected to the mafia. Even though I was well-dressed, albeit very bloody, the desk sergeant couldn't see beyond his preconceptions.

I went into the men's room at the station, and I remember looking at my face in the mirror and saying to myself "Oh God!" My eyes were already swollen, there were streaks of blood all over, my hair was matted with blood, and I was missing a couple of teeth. I knew it would be tough to get to a hospital—there were no cabs, and no one had telephones at that time. So I walked all the rest of the way home, about a mile.

When he learned what had happened to his son, Peter's father was outraged and sought redress from the Commissioner of Police. However, rather than contacting a lawyer, he took the advice of a young man who was involved in community affairs. This young man became an intermediary and asked that Peter's father meet with the policeman in question. The policeman—who had four children and who would lose his job if Peter's father pursued his complaint—came to the Rodino home, acknowledged that he had been under the influence of liquor, apologized, and agreed to take care of the bill to fix Peter's teeth. He got his teeth fixed, but as far as he knew the bill was never paid.[15]

This wanton act of discrimination was indelibly etched in Peter's memory. After all, he had been brought up to believe that the police upheld the law. During his forty years in Congress he consistently championed people who found themselves in situations where they would otherwise have no voice. He did this regardless of whether they were constituents. For instance, during the cold war Peter became involved with helping displaced persons gain asylum in the United States, people who had fled from communist-dominated countries and who would be persecuted if they returned. As a member of the Judiciary Committee's Immigration Subcommittee, he was in a unique position to effect enactment of private legislation that would advance the cause of such asylum-seekers. At the time, Peter was a strong anti-communist, a position that evolved from his own early experiences.

Before the Depression, Peter had attended Dana College, a two-year preparatory school where he studied philosophy, government and English. Many of his professors were liberal, and professed the idea that our government perpetuated a class system. When he graduated from Dana in 1929 he had used up his savings, the Depression had begun, and it was difficult to find work. The trade union movement had begun, and Peter, viewing himself as aligned with the working class, was attracted to the ideas of fringe groups like the American League against War and Fascism and the Young Federalists, which spoke about the need to break down the class system, to establish equality and provide more opportunity, particularly for blacks. After a time Peter received invitations to secret meetings that focused on the need to bring about changes in the system. His oratorical skills were recognized, and he was recruited as a speaker. He had vivid memories of standing on soap boxes, denouncing inequity and injustice on the streets around Branch Brook Park.

When Peter was invited to attend secret indoctrination classes, he began having second thoughts. As he told me, "the speakers, trained by extremists, told us that the day would come when the people would rise up against the government and man the barricades." Bloody revolution was not for Peter. "I decided then and there that I would have nothing more to do with them."

While attending University of Newark Law School and then serving in the army during World War II, Peter became deeply grateful to the United States for upholding freedom of expression and respect for human rights. He told me a story about his efforts on behalf of two nurses from Burma, Ruby Thaw and Hla Sein. They had been on the staff of Dr. Gordon Seagrave's famed Burma Hospital, caring for American and Allied wounded during World War II. In 1942, given a chance to flee from advancing Japanese troops to the safety of their native villages, the nurses remained with the Allies and walked with General Joseph Stilwell during a perilous twenty-six-day retreat from Burma. Later they returned to the front lines in the Burmese jungle and provided nursing care under the most dangerous conditions.

After the war Thaw and Sein came to the United States

on student visas to study obstetrics at Jersey City Medical Center. When their visas were about to expire, they faced a dilemma. Because they had given so much help to American soldiers during the war, they would now be considered traitors by the then-communist regime in Burma. Going home meant certain death.

A reporter for the *Newark Star-Ledger,* John McDowell, who had been wounded in the Burmese theater and cared for by Thaw and Sein, recognized their names in a list of people facing deportation. McDowell called upon Peter, his congressman, for help. Peter contacted the head of the immigration office in Newark and endorsed the nurses' application for a six-month visa extension. He then introduced a private bill authorizing permanent residency for the nurses and garnered support from members of the Judiciary Committee. The committee favorably reported out the bill, which subsequently became law. Later, Ruby Thaw wrote Peter to tell him that she had married an American citizen. Another letter followed a couple of years later, informing him that she had given birth to a baby boy and named him Peter.

Another case that stood out in Peter's mind involved a young man named John Hvasta, a veteran of World War II who, with his parents, had immigrated to the United States from Czechoslovakia. In 1948 Hvasta obtained a visa to study in Czechoslovakia under the GI Bill of Rights. Less than a month after he arrived there, the communists took over the country. Hvasta continued to pursue his studies and also got a job with the U.S. Consulate General. After being spotted taking photographs, he was accused of spying and given a three-year prison sentence. When he appealed, it turned into a ten-year sentence.

A priest who heard about John Hvasta's plight from his brother contacted Peter for assistance. Though the Hvasta family lived in a district other than Peter's, he was so moved that he started a concerted campaign to free Hvasta. Art Heenan, the city editor of the *Newark Star-Ledger*, helped keep the story before the public eye. Peter called upon veterans' groups for support and introduced a bill, which was assigned to the Foreign Affairs Committee, calling for sanctions against Czechoslovakia if Hvasta wasn't released.

Another American—native-born William Oatis, an Associated Press reporter—had also been arrested by the Czech government. The State Department had intervened and Oatis was freed. Because no action was being taken for Hvasta, Peter challenged the State Department. He ultimately met with both Presidents Truman and Eisenhower to express his indignation that Hvasta, as a naturalized American, wasn't being given the same treatment as a native-born American. In 1952 there were reports that Hvasta had escaped from prison. Peter's scrapbooks are filled with newspaper accounts of his relentless campaign on Hvasta's behalf, including getting the State Department to utilize the Voice of America to broadcast appeals to the Czech underground to search for and help Hvasta. Finally, after twenty-one months on the run from the Czech secret police, Hvasta sought asylum in the American embassy in Prague. The American ambassador negotiated with the Czech authorities to secure his release, and in February 1954 he returned home.

Regarding Hvasta's return, Peter commented, "There is a great struggle today between two different ways of life. One—the tradition of Western civilization—holds that the individual and his liberties are of prime importance; the state exists for him…. We set no price on a human life, nor do we spare any effort to save it. The case of John Hvasta is a gratifying example of the importance of each citizen to the government of the United States."[16]

Civil rights was another area where Peter demonstrated his deep commitment to the "fundamental American dream that all men are created equal, and that equal opportunity for a better life should be within the reach of all." His predecessor as chairman of the House Judiciary Committee, the esteemed Emanuel Celler, referred to Peter as his right arm. As such, and later as chairman, Peter helped guide every civil rights bill through the arduous twists and turns of the political process in the House.

In 1963 President Kennedy invited several members of the Judiciary Committee to a meeting at the White House, including Peter and Speaker John McCormack, another of his mentors. They were to discuss how to reconcile differences about what should be included in—and how to ensure Republican support for—the pending Civil Rights

Act. This landmark bill was to prohibit discrimination on the basis of race, color, religion, sex and national origin in the areas of voting, employment, education and public accommodations. Peter was adamant that a section prohibiting discrimination in employment be included in the bill. What good was giving equality to minorities if you didn't also do it economically? When it was his turn to speak, he voiced his opinion to President Kennedy about the importance of a strong section on equal employment opportunity. If the administration did not support this proposal, he would bring it to the House floor as an amendment.

"Now wait a minute, Peter," Speaker McCormack interrupted, concerned that the president might mistake these words for a challenge.

But the president just said, "Don't worry, Peter, we'll go along with that."

This provision, which Peter authored, became Title VII of the historic Civil Rights Act of 1964. "This bill is founded upon those same principles which have formed the cornerstone of our democratic government from the very beginning," Peter said in his remarks on the House floor in support of the act.

> Even before our Constitution was adopted, the leaders of the American Revolution created a ringing statement of belief, a declaration of conscience which told the world

how Americans felt about people and their governments.

As we debate this bill, I hope all of us will keep in mind these stirring words from the Declaration of Independence: "We hold these truths to be self-evident, that all men are created equal, that they are endowed by their Creator with certain unalienable rights, that among these are life, liberty, and the pursuit of happiness." It is up to us, 188 years later, to assure to all Americans these unalienable rights.[17]

Likewise, Peter played a key role in the enactment of the Voting Rights Act of 1965, which carried out the mandate of the Fifteenth Amendment.

In 1973, when the Leaguers, a New Jersey community organization, gave Peter their Man of the Year award, Congressman Robert Nix of Pennsylvania provided a tribute that sums up Peter's lifelong commitment to ensuring that each individual be afforded equal treatment under the law: "He is truly the kind of American whose entire life reflects the principles upon which this country was founded.... Peter Rodino is at heart neither white nor black; he is one of those rare individuals who is a part of every man of every race and who diligently gives of his energies and intellectual capabilities to uphold right and justice for all men."[18]

Brigadier General Thoburn Brown presenting Peter with the
Bronze Star Medal for meritorious achievement, 1945.
(U.S. Signal Corps, Peter W. Rodino, Jr., Papers,
Seton Hall University School of Law)

Rodino campaign headquarters in Newark, around 1946.
(AZ Photo Service, Rodino Papers)

With Eleanor Roosevelt during Peter's 1946 campaign.
(George Van, courtesy of *The Star-Ledger*, Rodino Papers)

Campaign event, 1948.
(AZ Photo Service, Rodino Papers)

Campaigning with President Truman in 1952.
(George Van, courtesy of *The Star-Ledger*, Rodino Papers)

Campaigning at a factory in 1954.
(Ace Alagna, courtesy of the *Italian Tribune*, Rodino Papers)

Campaign motorcade, 1954.
(Ace Alagna, courtesy of the *Italian Tribune*, Rodino Papers)

Peter with his father and father's co-workers.
(North Jersey Press and Commercial Photo, Rodino Papers)

At a public event, 1956.
(*Newark News*, courtesy of The Newark Public Library, Rodino Papers)

With President Kennedy and Vice President Johnson.
(Ace Alagna, courtesy of the *Italian Tribune*, Rodino Papers)

Standing next to Martin Luther King, Jr., as President Johnson
signs the 1964 Civil Rights Act.
(Cecil Stoughton, LBJ Library)

Demonstration at the 1972 Democratic National Convention
supporting Peter for vice-presidential nomination.
(Rodino Papers)

Greeting a constituent during 1972 campaign.
(Rodino Papers)

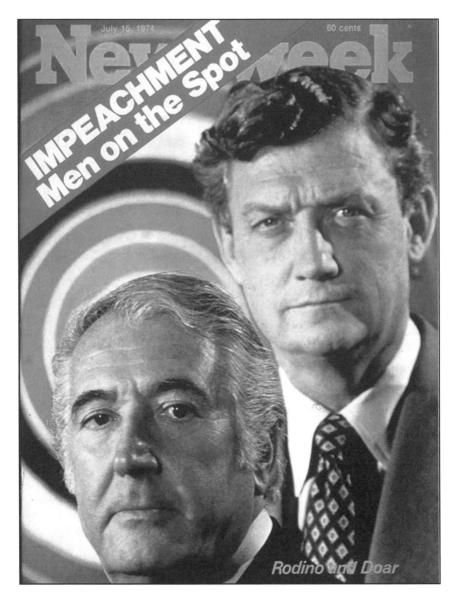

July 15, 1974.   60 cents

Newsweek

IMPEACHMENT
Men on the Spot

Rodino and Doar

Cover of *Newsweek* Magazine, July 15, 1974.

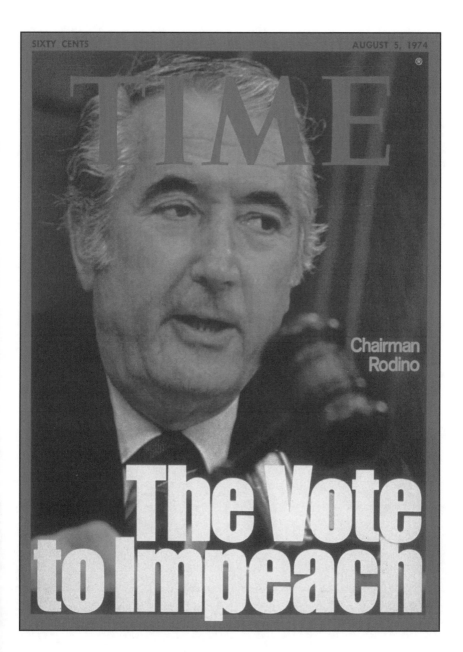

SIXTY CENTS AUGUST 5, 1974

TIME

®

Chairman
Rodino

The Vote
to Impeach

Cover of *TIME* Magazine, August 5, 1974.
Permission from Time Magazine © 2008 Time, Inc.

Press photographers during impeachment proceedings.
(Dev O'Neill, Rodino Papers)

Delivering the final Impeachment Inquiry Report to House Majority
Leader Tip O'Neill, August 20, 1974.
(Dev O'Neill, Rodino Papers)

Southern Christian Leadership Conference annual convention, 1976, during which Peter received the Martin Luther King, Jr., Award. (Courtesy of the SCLC, Rodino Papers)

Discussing Judiciary Committee issues
with Senator Ted Kennedy, 1978.
(Rodino Papers)

Being awarded the Grand Cross of the Order of Merit of the Republic of Italy. Peter is congratulated by the Italian ambassador, Egidio Ortona, as Speaker of the House John McCormack looks on. (Rodino Papers)

Grand Marshal of the Columbus Day Parade in Chicago, 1974.
(Rodino Papers)

Conferring with President Carter in the Oval Office.
(Courtesy of the Jimmy Carter Library, Rodino Papers)

Unveiling of Peter's portrait in the House Judiciary Committee
hearing room, May 1977 (front row: Representatives Barbara Jordan
and Robert Drinan; back row: Peter, Vice President Walter Mondale,
Majority Leader Tip O'Neill).
(Rodino Papers)

PROVIDE FOR
THE COMMON DEFENSE

One of the most compelling arguments for a solid federal union was that it would be "indispensable to providing for the common defense."[19] Under the new Constitution, the federal government, not individual states, would be responsible for national security. That responsibility, of course, posed questions about possible clashes between the federal government's power and the power of the people.

One of the early questions the Founding Fathers faced was whether there should be any limitations on the power of the federal government to maintain a standing military force in peacetime. Opposition to peacetime armies arose from those who wanted no restrictions placed on the people's liberty.[20] James Madison, in Federalist #41, answered the opponents: "How could a readiness for war in time of peace be safely prohibited unless we could prohibit, in like manner, the preparations and establishments of every hostile nation?"[21]

The framers of the Constitution established separation of powers and a system of checks and balances to protect against possible abuse by the federal government of its war power. While the civilian president was commander-in-chief, Congress would be responsible for military appropriations, and they would have to be re-enacted every two years; Congress was given the power to declare war; presidential treaties would have to be ratified by the Senate.[22] The framers had no way of predicting the power of the modern presidency and the vast and costly military-industrial establishment that would take root in the twentieth century. Over the years, the system of checks and balances has often failed to rein in the power of the federal government during wartime. One of the most prominent examples of the federal government's abuse of civil liberties during wartime is the confinement of Japanese-Americans in internment camps during World War II.[23] As chairman of the Judiciary Committee, Peter strongly supported passage of the Civil Liberties Act of 1988, by which the United States formally apologized to the Japanese-American community and paid reparations to internees and their heirs.

Peter was adamant that the military be used for defense, not aggression. Deeply dismayed by the United States' incursion into Iraq in 2003, he contrasted the situation faced by reserve troops being called up to serve in that effort with his own decision to enlist in the army in March of 1941.

As an appeals agent for his local draft board, Peter was automatically exempt from the draft. However, feeling a strong duty to serve, he enlisted for what was then a one-year tour of duty, turning down an opportunity to go to officer candidate school and instead being assigned to Fort Dupont in Delaware. At the time Peter was dating his future wife, Ann Stango. On December 7, 1941, she arrived in Wilmington by train and they went to dinner at the Dupont Hotel. Peter, almost thirty-two years old at the time, had just been advised that soldiers over the age of twenty-nine would be eligible for discharge. As they were discussing their future, a radio in the restaurant started crackling with the news of the Japanese attack on Pearl Harbor. Sirens began to wail and bullhorns blared in the streets: "All military personnel, return to quarters. This is an emergency, return to your quarters!"

As Peter recounted, "I took Ann to the train. She was distraught, and I tried to reassure her that things would be all right. And then I said, 'We're going to get married anyhow—will you marry me?' Ann said yes and I put her on the train. Our hearts were aching. It was such a sad farewell."

He and Ann decided to get married as soon as possible. On December 27, 1941, they were married at the Immaculate Conception Church in Wilmington, and the following January Peter was assigned to Jacksonville, Florida. In

March he was sent to Indian Town Gap, Pennsylvania, a staging area for troops going overseas. By this time Ann was pregnant, and Peter recounted how difficult it was knowing that he wouldn't be present for the birth. After the baby was born, he received a telegram from his father saying "baby born." "I had previously made up my mind that our child was going to be a boy," he told me, "and so I of course assumed it was a boy. I passed around cigars and told everyone I had a son. Because mail delivery overseas was so erratic, it wasn't until months later that I learned that I was the father of a girl! That was when I received my first photograph of her, and I remember marveling at how beautiful she was."

Peter's unit—the Second Army Corps, First Armored Division—was one of the first American troops to land in Britain. Shortly thereafter he and about forty others received orders to go to officer candidate school in Cheltenham, an intensive three-month training program for "the West Pointers of America in England." Peter emerged a second lieutenant and subsequently received orders to report to the Intelligence Division, Headquarters Company, in North Africa. After about a year and a half there, Peter had accumulated enough time overseas to be eligible for a rotation home, but his knowledge of French and Italian being critical to the war effort, instead he remained on active duty. A joint British-American force was taking shape, the Military Mission Italian Army (MMIA). Peter applied, received his acceptance, and was soon making his way to a replacement depot in Naples to await further orders.

While in Naples, Peter recounted, he had a close call. His brother-in-law George had gotten a pass and gone to visit him. "We were sleeping in a tent, on cots, when the air raid sirens started blaring and we heard the sounds of artillery firing. We ran outside to try to get to a shelter, but before we had gotten very far, we heard a *thud* and a bomb dropped to the ground a few feet away. I definitely felt the hand of God protecting us when it turned out to be a dud!"

Shortly after the bomb scare, in the middle of the night, he was awakened by a flashlight. A corporal said he was looking for one Lieutenant Rodino, who had orders to report to a tank destroyer battalion. Wasting no time, Peter reported to the commanding officer and told him about his verbal orders to join the MMIA. He had already spent time in a fighting unit. The colonel, showing little sympathy, told him to clear it through the channels. Knowing that would take a long time, he walked away dejected, picturing himself in a body bag.

"At that moment," he said, "I passed an office identified as Classification and Assignment. I peered inside and recognized a friend. We had come overseas on the liberty boat together." The man, now a major, greeted him by saying, "God, are you still just a lieutenant?" When Peter told him his predicament, the major tore up his orders and promptly wrote up new ones to MMIA. Peter asked him how he was supposed to travel there. "I'm going to lend you a jeep," his friend replied. "Put your ass in it and don't stop till you get to Rome!"

Peter felt as if he had been blessed once again. As he told me, "My linguistic skills were quickly put to use, and I was given the opportunity to act as adjutant to the commanding general of Rome." In addition to carrying out the general's orders, Peter took charge of all Allied logistics in Rome. This presented him with wonderful opportunities. He met the king of Italy and other members of the royal family as well as various leading lights in Rome, and he had a chance to hone his political skills. In December of 1945, almost five years after enlisting, Peter finally returned home as a decorated captain.

The Founding Fathers could never have imagined that the United States, in providing for the common defense, would engage in a conflict as global as World War II, one that so completely mobilized the nation. In unprecedented numbers, men and women answered the call to sacrifice for their nation's defense. As one of "we the people," Peter served his nation well.

PROMOTE THE
GENERAL WELFARE

In several cases handed down in 1936 and 1937, during the Great Depression, the Supreme Court defined the scope of the phrase "to promote the general welfare." In *United States v. Butler* (1936), the court settled differences of opinion among the Founding Fathers as to whether this phrase should be interpreted narrowly or broadly by finding that Congress had the power to authorize the spending of money "to cover anything conducive to national welfare." In two other cases, based on the decision in *Butler*, the court upheld the constitutionality of sections of the Social Security Act of 1935 authorizing federal assistance for unemployment compensation and old-age pensions.[24]

In his State of the Union address in 1944, President Franklin D. Roosevelt expanded the concept of the general welfare by his vision of postwar peace:

It is our duty now to begin to lay the plans and determine the strategy for the winning of a lasting peace and the establishing of an American standard of living higher than ever before known. We cannot be content, no matter how high that general standard of living may be, if some fraction of our people—whether it be one-third or one-fifth or one-tenth—is ill-fed, ill-clothed, ill-housed, and insecure....

We have come to a clear realization of the fact that true individual freedom cannot exist without economic security and independence.[25]

During his forty years in Congress, Peter consistently supported legislation to promote the general welfare in the broadest sense, in alignment with his belief that the government should do for the people what they couldn't do for themselves. His was a strong voice on behalf of fair housing legislation and legal services for the poor; he stood in the forefront of the congressional effort to stem drug abuse; and he authored landmark anti-trust legislation to protect consumers.

From the time Peter first entered Congress in 1949, he championed reform of the country's "discriminatory, inflexible and inequitable" immigration policy, the national origins quota system. That policy gave large quotas to western European countries, curbed migration from southern and eastern European countries, and stringently restricted migration from the Far East. As an Italian-American and a member of the Judiciary Committee's Immigration and Nationality Subcommittee, Peter was particularly sensitive to the plight of people with family in the United States who had to wait years before immigrating to the United States, while large quotas given to some European countries were going unused. In a speech in 1965 he urged passage of legislation repealing such an unjust system. "This long overdue change," Peter said,

> recognizes the dignity of the individual and is predicated on the principle that one person is no less desirable than any other person regardless of his race or place of birth.... We know that immigration is good for the country in terms of national wealth, national culture, national productivity and national defense.
>
> Surely one of the greatest sources of the strength of America is to be found in the diversity of the groups making up our nation. Each group has brought its traditions, its culture, its individual genius, and these in turn have become part of the American heritage. Diversity marks the various contributions to this heritage; unity has been the outgrowth of a shared experience, of shared values. The

American nation today stands as eloquent
proof that there is no inherent contradiction
between unity and diversity.[26]

Peter was also instrumental in the passage of the
Immigration Reform and Control Act of 1986, popularly
known as Simpson-Rodino. This legislation—the culmi-
nation of recommendations by the Select Commission on
Immigration and Refugee Policy, a blue-ribbon panel of
sixteen members representing Congress, the administration and the public—provided amnesty for some three
million undocumented workers who could prove they
had been in the United States since 1982, together with
employer sanctions for hiring undocumented workers. A
major obstacle to enactment of similar legislation in the
prior Congress had been the lack of adequate funding
support from the administration. Peter had Senator Alan
Simpson, Republican from Wyoming and one of the bill's
co-sponsors, arrange for Peter to meet with President
Reagan at the White House. During their conversation
Peter told President Reagan that if the bill were enacted,
it would require a commitment of a billion dollars a
year, and that Peter would not move forward without the
president's support. According to Peter, Reagan turned
to his budget director, Jim Miller, and asked him if they
could find that amount in the budget. Finally, Peter had
his commitment. Subsequently, Secretary of the Treasury

Donald Regan offered Peter the help of his department in securing its passage.

Peter found it amusing—and also touching—to learn later that many of the migrants whose lives were dramatically affected by this legislation often referred to themselves as *los Rodinos*. It was a fitting tribute to this man of the people.

SECURE THE BLESSINGS OF LIBERTY TO OURSELVES AND OUR POSTERITY

During the grave constitutional crisis of 1974, Peter often said, he turned to the Preamble for inspiration. He thought hard about the kind of government our forefathers left to us—a democratic way of life founded upon a constitution and governed by the rule of law—and concluded that, as the people's representative, it was his job above all to preserve for posterity the blessings of liberty. "That concept," he explained to me,

> Permeates our history, beginning with the Declaration of Independence, when Thomas Jefferson affirmed that we are endowed by our creator "with certain unalienable rights," that among them are "life, liberty and the pursuit of happiness." Then there is the reference

at the conclusion of the Preamble "to secure the blessings of liberty to ourselves and our posterity." And finally, the Gettysburg Address reaffirms that "our nation is conceived in liberty, and dedicated to the proposition that all men are created equal."

The blessings of liberty—they are at the core of our constitutional rights, our Bill of Rights—the right to speak out freely, the right of freedom of religion, the right to equality, to justice, to freely assemble. But with those rights there are also responsibilities—as contained in the command of the Preamble "to secure the blessings of liberty to ourselves and our posterity."

When I asked Peter what some of our responsibilities were, he replied that we should respect the rights of others, work for the betterment of our fellow beings, and participate in government, demanding integrity in our leaders and our institutions and holding them accountable.

"As beneficiaries of the blessings of liberty," Peter told his students, "we must be ever vigilant and ever mindful of the wise words of Benjamin Franklin, who, when asked, 'What kind of government do we have?' replied, 'A republic, if you can keep it.'" Peter impressed on his students the importance of sustaining the republic by exercising our most precious right, the right to vote, dedicating ourselves to the sanctity of the rule of law, and upholding the high ideals upon which our nation was founded.

For my husband, the Constitution was a perpetually evolving document, a set of ideals toward which we should constantly aspire. No one gave more eloquent testimony to that concept than Congresswoman Barbara Jordan, a member of the Judiciary Committee, in her famous remarks during the Nixon impeachment debate. When the Constitution was completed in 1787, she noted, as an African-American woman she was not considered one of "we the people." It was only "through the process of amendment, interpretation and court decision" that the government finally recognized her status as a citizen with full rights. Peter shared her heartfelt sentiment that "[m]y faith in the Constitution is whole, it is complete, it is total."[27] In 2008, that unwavering faith found it's full expression in the historic election of our first African-American president.

Toward the end of his life, Peter received an e-mail with the subject heading "What Will Matter" that asked this question: "How will the value of your days be measured?" Moved by a message that summed up the essence of his beliefs, Peter quoted it in all the speeches he gave from that point on. It went like this:

> What will matter is not what you bought but what you built; not what you got, but what you gave.

What will matter is not your success, but your significance.

What will matter is not what you learned, but what you taught.

What will matter is every act of integrity, compassion, courage or sacrifice that enriched, empowered or encouraged others to emulate your example.

What will matter is not your competence, but your character....

Living a life that matters doesn't happen by accident.

It's not a matter of circumstance, but of choice.

Peter exhorted his students to "choose to live a life that matters."[28]

I can think of no more fitting way to describe Peter's life. He was a prime example of his own advice—a man of integrity, compassion, courage and sacrifice, who lived a life that mattered. His dedication to fostering bipartisanship in Congress, and the honorable and principled life he led, serve as examples for leaders in today's troubled times.

When growing up, the first thing Peter saw in the morning through his bedroom window and the last thing he saw at night were two huge elm trees in Branch Brook Park. They reminded him of two giant arms reaching out to the sky. He recalled how those trees became a focus of contemplation for him, mirroring his quest for answers about his destiny, his reaching out to discover the higher purpose in his life.

Looking back on his public life in later years, Peter highlighted two achievements that were the most fulfilling to him personally. One was the landmark civil rights legislation that he shepherded to fruition and that gave new life to the Preamble's command that the government secure the blessings of liberty. The other was the bipartisan Judiciary Committee vote to impeach President Nixon. The simple yet profound principles by which Peter guided the committee—fairness and justice—had prevailed. After the vote, but before the matter could be brought to the full House, the Supreme Court ordered that the president release to the committee subpoenaed tape recordings of conversations he had had in the Oval Office—one of which contained the so-called smoking gun, proof of obstruction of justice. Overnight, Nixon's political support vanished. Facing impeachment by the House and the likelihood of conviction by the Senate, the president resigned. The United States had survived its greatest test as a democracy.

Upon Peter's passing, Ted Kennedy, the Democratic senator from Massachusetts, said that during the Watergate inquiry, "Many of us felt that we were seeing a Founding Father in action, living the highest ideals of the

Constitution. I'm sure my brother would have called him a profile in courage. I feel the same way."[29]

Those words deeply touched my heart. I don't believe Peter's reverence for the Preamble could have been greater had he been one of the Founding Fathers. I will be forever grateful for the years I was blessed to spend with him, and for the way his vision expanded my own. Thank you, Peter, for teaching me to see through your eyes.

NOTES

1. Cornel Nistorescu, "Ode to America," Evenimentul Zilei, Sept. 24, 2001. Available at http://www.evz.ro/article. php?artid=74704.
2. Debate on Articles of Impeachment: Hearing on H. Res. 803 before the House Committee on the Judiciary, 93rd Cong. 4 (1974), statement of Rep. Peter W. Rodino, Jr., committee chairman.
3. Peter W. Rodino, Jr., "The Compact with the People," 27 Santa Clara Law Review 1987, 471-74.
4. Oral history tapes, Peter W. Rodino, Jr., Papers, AV-016, 9, AV-015, 20, Seton Hall University School of Law.
5. Oral history tape, Rodino Papers, AV-015, 7.
6. Id.
7. Id.
8. 120 Congressional Record 2, 2350 (1974).
9. Id. at 2351.
10. Oral history tape, Rodino Papers, AV-015, 7.
11. Id.
12. House Committee on the Judiciary, Impeachment of Richard M. Nixon, President of the United States, H.R. Doc. No. 93-339 at 6 (1974).
13. Id. at 7.
14. Oral history tape, Rodino Papers, AV-015, 11.

15. Id., AV-015, 13.
16. 100 Cong. Rec. 2, 2008 (1954).
17. 110 Cong. Rec. 2, 1539 (1964).
18 Letter from Congressman Robert N.C. Nix, 2nd District, Pennsylvania, to Constance Woodruff of the Leaguers, Dec. 10, 1973, Rodino Papers, PER-076, 13.
19. Mortimer J. Adler and William Gorman, The American Testament 92 (Praeger Publishers, 1975).
20. Id. at 93-94.
21. Id. at 94.
22. Id. at 96-97.
23. Id. at 99-100.
24. Id. at 103-5.
25. Id. at 106.
26. 111 Cong. Rec. 16, 21594 (1965).
27. Debate on Articles of Impeachment: Hearing on H. Res. 803 before the H. Comm. on the Judiciary, 93rd Cong. 111 (1974), statement of Rep. Barbara Jordan.
28. Michael Josephson, "What Will Matter," weekly commentary from Michael Josephson, October 6–10, 2003, no. 4, http://charactercounts.org/knxwk 326.htm.
29. Letter from Senator Edward M. Kennedy to Joy Rodino, May 16, 2005, Rodino Papers, PER-190, 3.